W9-CBU-184

WEBSITE DESIGN

Cavendish
Square

New York

Kezia
Endsley

To Piper, Christopher, and Ryan with love.

Published in 2015 by Cavendish Square Publishing, LLC
243 5th Avenue, Suite 136, New York, NY 10016

First Edition

Website: cavendishsq.com

This publication represents the opinions and views of the author based on his or her personal experience, knowledge, and research. The information in this book serves as a general guide only. The author and publisher have used their best efforts in preparing this book and disclaim liability rising directly or indirectly from the use and application of this book.

CPSIA Compliance Information: Batch #WW15CSQ

All websites were available and accurate when this book was sent to press.

Library of Congress Cataloging-in-Publication Data

Endsley, Kezia, 1968- author.
Website design / Kezia Endsley.
pages cm. — (High-tech jobs)
Includes bibliographical references and index.
ISBN 978-1-50260-111-7 (hardcover) — ISBN 978-1-50260-109-4 (ebook)
1. Web site development—Vocational guidance. 2. Web sites—Design—Vocational guidance. I. Title.

TK5105.888.E535 2015
006.7023—dc23

2014015956

Editor: Kristen Susienka
Copy Editor: Cynthia Roby
Art Director: Jeffrey Talbot
Senior Designer: Amy Greenan
Senior Production Manager: Jennifer Ryder-Talbot
Production Editor: David McNamara
Photo Researcher: J8 Media

The photographs in this book are used by permission and through the courtesy of: Cover photo and 1, asharkyu/Shutterstock.com; Droidworker/Shutterstock.com, 4; Saranai/Shutterstock.com, 8; everythingpossible/iStock/Thinkstock, 10; Piotr Adamowicz/Shutterstock.com, 12; Noah Seelam/AFP/Getty Images, 13; Amy Greenan for Cavendish Square,14; David Paul Morris/Getty Images, 15; Seyyahil/Shutterstock.com, 17; mediaphotos/E+/Getty Images, 19; © NetPhotos/Alamy, 28; michaeljung/iStock/Thinkstock, 35; © Andres Rodriguez/Alamy, 36; -Oxford-/E+/Getty Images, 37; Piotr Adamowicz/Shutterstock.com, 38; Nielsen Norman Group, 41; lana rinck/Shutterstock.com, 42; exdez/iStock Vectors/Getty Images, 44; Kate Pru/Shutterstock.com, 47; 4774344sean/iStock/Thinkstock, 48; ronstik/Shutterstock.com, 52; © iStockphoto.com/fazon1, 53; bloomua/Shutterstock.com, 56; David Bjorgen/File:Smithsonian Castle Doorway.jpg/Wikimedia Commons, 61; g-stockstudio/Shutterstock.com, 62; scyther5/iStock/Thinkstock, 67; Jcomp/iStock/Thinkstock, 68; phasinphoto/iStock/Thinkstock, 71; © AP Images/Mary Altaffer, 74; mariakraynova/Shutterstock.com, 75; MaleWitch/iStock/Thinkstock, 77; buchachon/iStock/Thinkstock, 79.

Printed in the United States of America

CONTENTS

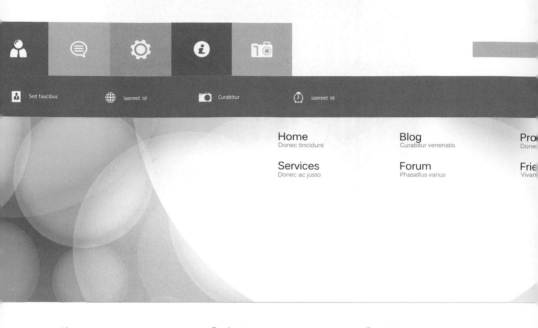

Home
Donec tincidunt

Blog
Curabitur venenatis

Pro
Done

Services
Donec ac justo

Forum
Phasellus varius

Frie
Vivan

Sed faucibus   laoreet id   Curabitur   laoreet id

About   Projects   Contact

Lorem ipsum dolor.   Aenean id aliquet arcu.   Nullam pulvinar congue.

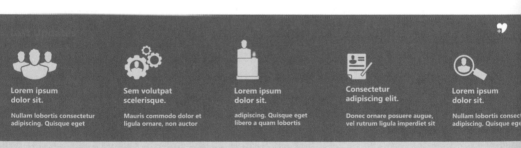

Lorem ipsum dolor sit.

Nullam lobortis consectetur
adipiscing. Quisque eget

Sem volutpat
scelerisque.

Mauris commodo dolor et
ligula ornare, non auctor

Lorem ipsum
dolor sit.

adipiscing. Quisque eget
libero a quam lobortis

Consectetur
adipiscing elit.

Donec ornare posuere augue,
vel rutrum ligula imperdiet sit

Lorem ipsum
dolor sit.

Nullam lobortis consect
adipiscing. Quisque ege

Website design is a creative and lucrative career with a future.

INTRODUCTION TO WEBSITE DESIGN

What exactly is website design? What exactly do website designers do on the job, day in and day out? What kinds of skills and educational background do you need to succeed in this field? How much can you expect to make, and what are the pros and cons of this field? Does this career path have a future? Is it even the right career for you?

This book can help you answer these and other questions by explaining what website designers do, how to prepare for the field, how to break into the field, and how to become a successful website designer. Website design is, in fact, a lucrative and enjoyable career with a future. It's also a very competitive field, and this book can be your first step in preparing to smash your competition!

WEBSITE DESIGN: BORN OF CHAOS

Website design is a relative newcomer to the world of design, if you consider that humans have been designing spaces and objects since they were able to communicate abstractly, which developed around the same time that language did. Website design borrows from the basic principles of all effective designs and adapts these techniques for the unique environment of the screen.

Website design has reinvented itself many times in the past few decades, as bandwidths and users' expectations have grown. When the Internet was in its infancy, website design was almost nonexistent. Websites then were about providing users with as much text-based information as possible, with few design details. Anything "fancy," such as an image, could cause annoying and unacceptable download delays. Those first so-called "designers" used various fonts and all caps to differentiate between concepts and sections. It was chaos, via text.

As cross-platform technologies (which can be used on any computer, regardless of its underlying platform) advanced and bandwidths increased, many traditional designers saw an untapped market and were drawn in by the idea of designing for the web. At first, this primarily meant designing the front end of the website by using **HTML (Hypertext Markup Language)** markup code, and its various cousins, in order to create a pleasing experience for the users. The development of browsers like Mosaic that could handle graphics meant that designers could begin to design for a more visual experience.

As happens with all evolving phenomena, there came a need to develop other areas of design and organization. Website design gradually became a deeper issue, addressing how the whole site was designed for maximum efficiency, ease-of-use, and for a pleasurable user experience.

HOW THE CAREER HAS EVOLVED

Today, modern website design includes many interrelated disciplines that are involved in creating and maintaining websites. The different areas of web design include **web graphic design**, **interface design**, **user experience design**, and **search engine optimization**. Consider each of these more closely:

- Web graphic design focuses on the graphical elements of a website, including web page layout. Website designers use **Cascading Style Sheets (CSS)**, **JavaScript** code, and HTML markup tags to design and organize websites for viewers.

- Interface design helps two or more components of a system connect and communicate effectively. Interface designers focus their talents on creating user interfaces that are simple and efficient, with a special focus on understanding and designing for interfaces, such as forms and data-entry displays. This is also called "user-centered design."

- User experience design focuses on traditional human–computer interaction, and extends it by addressing all aspects of a product or service as perceived by its users. Designers who focus on user-experience design, which includes but isn't limited to designing the interface, take an all-encompassing approach. The focus is on the users' emotions when they interact with the design, in the hope of creating a pleasurable experience.

- Search engine optimization positively affects the visibility of a website in a search engine's "natural," or unpaid, search results. SEO designers consider how search engines such as Google work, as well as what people search for, and design and edit content and coding so that the site will appear higher ranked on aw search results page.

“ ”

A website without SEO
is like a car with no gas.

PAUL COOKSON,
WEB DESIGNER AND AUTHOR

Creating an effective interface involves simple and efficient effects that entice viewers to stay on your website.

Each of these areas has grown from the original idea of website design as the needs and wants of users have evolved. If you are interested in website design but you don't know which field is best for you, you're reading the right book. You'll learn more about each area, including the skills and education necessary to excel in them, as well as the outlook of each career in the near future.

A CAREER OF CHANGE

Website design is a very competitive yet thriving career path. Someone who develops and massages content for the web can count on having a job in the long foreseeable future, even though the nature of that job is sure to change, and change again, in the decades that follow. One thing you should be sure of before you

> ## Intuitive design is how we give the user new superpowers.

JARED SPOOL,
*WEB SITE USABILITY:
A DESIGNER'S GUIDE*

pursue a career in website design is that you are comfortable with, and welcome, change. The field of website design will morph many times over during your lifetime, and you need to be open and ready to grow and change along with it.

WHERE SHOULD YOU START?

Today's Internet begs a fundamental question of all good designers: not what can they do, but what should they do? Designers are no longer held hostage by bandwidth or cross-platform issues, so they have free rein to create as their visions demand. With that freedom comes responsibility. In order to design well, you need to understand the basics of good design.

As with all design, it's critical to keep the users in mind. The best designers know who they are designing for, and understand how to translate that specific audience's needs and desires into a great user experience.

If this is a challenge that sounds fun and exciting to you, you're in the right place. Read on!

The first step to a great design is understanding what your users want and need.

Website Design

A CAREER
1 IN WEBSITE
DESIGN: THE
BIG PICTURE

B ecoming a professional website designer isn't just about being able to make attractive, functional, and relevant web pages. It's also about organizing a site, creating interfaces that are easy to use and understand, being able to use and be comfortable with technologies such as HTML, JavaScript, and CSS, and being able to adapt your designs and coding for different media. It's about understanding what your audience wants and needs and knowing how to translate that into a design, making sure your site can be read by Google so people can find it when they search for it. Creating a website is a multi-step process, and web designers are involved in each of the steps.

Some degree of artistic talent, creativity, and imagination is also needed. Luckily, even if you do not feel that you are especially creative, you can get better. Just like many skills, you can improve your creativity and imagination by practicing. The more you try to think this way, the easier it will become.

```
<![endif...
<meta http-equiv... co...
<meta name="author" co...
<meta name="description" conte...
<meta name="keywords" content="">
</head>
<body>
<div id="wrapper">
<div class="header columns">
<div class="column"><a href="/" title="Company"><img sr
"|.graphic/logotypes/company_logo.png" alt="Company"><
<div class="column last">
<form action="|search.html" id="search" name="se
"round"><input type="text" name="query" class="
"Type text to find"><input type="submit" clas
"Search"></form>
```

HTML is one of the most used computer languages.

Before you get too overwhelmed with all the things that web designers are supposed to know and do, take a closer look at how web design came about, and how it works today.

THE ORIGINS OF WEBSITE DESIGN

When websites were first introduced (around 1991, in the United States) they were largely and primarily globs of text. The idea of making it attractive or including graphics was not yet a possibility.

The web began with HTML, which is a text markup language that allows designers to code words (and later, graphics) with certain tags so that they appear with specific characteristics and styling. The idea was that regardless of which browser the viewer used, or which settings the user's computer were set to, the website would have a predictable and legible look. In fact, creating a consistent look across different browsers, media, and client-determined settings remains a challenge for website designers.

Fast-forward a few years and bandwidths were increasing. Users eventually replaced slow and clunky dial-up modems as they began accessing the web via faster broadband connections, which used wires or fiber optic cables. The now commonplace wireless broadband connections were still a few years away.

Quicker access meant that "new" technologies, such as the JavaScript programming language, the Adobe Flash player,

Tim Berners-Lee, British computer scientist and inventor of the World Wide Web.

and CSS, could be used to develop image-based and interactive websites. It wasn't until JavaScript came along in 1995 that websites could be dynamic and interactive. Initially JavaScript had a lot of bugs and didn't work too well with many of the browsers. Through trial and error, browsers such as Netscape and Mosaic became more compatible with later versions of Java Script.

JavaScript allows developers to create scripts that can interact with users and change the content that's displayed, depending on the user's settings and responses. Almost any time you see an interactive animation on a website, play a game, or enter information into a field, JavaScript is running.

JavaScript was seen as the brains behind the website's code, but it was the introduction of CSS that really influenced the look and style of web pages. The use of CSS as a way to consistently style websites was introduced in 1995 by the **World Wide Web Consortium (W3C)**. Style sheets afforded developers a

```
body    {       background-color: #fffffa;
                background-image: url('../images/kitten.jpg');
                background-repeat: repeat;
                font-family: Arial, Helvetica, sens-serif;
                margin-left: 40px;
                margin-right: 40px;
                margin-top: 40 px;
                margin-bottom: 40 px }

h1      {       font-family: Times, serif;
                font-size: x-large;   }

h2      {       font-family: serif;
                font-size: large;     }

p       {       line-height: 130%;
                align="left";  }

footer {        text-align: left;
                font-family: Arial, Helvetica, sens-serif;
                font-size: x-small;
                line-height: normal;
                font-style: italic    }
```

Cascading Style Sheets, like this one, are used to control the styles and layouts of webpages.

separation between the actual content of the website and the styling of it. Separating style from content enabled designers to provide more flexibility and control over how information was displayed, regardless of the browser the user was using. Style sheets, which are like templates, were also more efficient than previous styling efforts because they enabled many pages to share formatting aspects and allowed for repetitive structural content.

Modern-day CSS can even allow the same markup page to be presented in different styles for different rendering methods, such as on-screen, in print, by voice (when read by a speech-based browser or screen reader), and even on Braille-based, tactile devices.

Since their inceptions, JavaScript and CSS have continually been updated and each new version has brought with it new features and capabilities. For example, CSS3 introduced new and better ways for consistently handling and displaying color on

Steve Jobs unveils the Apple iPhone at MacWorld Expo in 2007.

websites. Web designers concentrated their efforts on keeping up with new versions and adding new features to their websites as they were introduced in new versions of JavaScript and CSS. This was the way things progressed until the introduction of smartphones and tablets.

ENTER SMARTPHONES AND TABLETS

Apple's introduction of the smartphone in 2007 paved the way for websites to be designed and developed for viewing on smaller devices. Previously, most people viewed websites from their laptops and desktops. In fact, the number of users accessing the web from mobile devices is growing rapidly, and is set to overtake desktop access by 2015. Cisco Systems Inc. predicts 50 percent growth year over year of mobile traffic from 2013 to 2018. That's important for designers to know, understand, and plan for.

Designing a website to be accessed and used on a smartphone requires a different approach from that of traditional web design. In addition to screen size limitations that designers weren't accustomed to dealing with, wireless broadband connections initially reined in the speed and reliability of the typical user's connection. In other words, cellular broadband was typically slower and less reliable than wire-based connections, and web designers needed to understand and accommodate those restrictions.

In all likelihood, you'll need to design your sites to look great and work well with all these platforms. One popular way to do this is through a technique called **responsive design**. In responsive design, the website recognizes which device viewers are using to access it, and it responds by providing the version of the website that's been designed just for that device. In fact, modern-day CSS can be used to allow the web page to display differently depending on the screen size or device on which it is being viewed.

If you're wondering why it's important to know the history of the web and website design, think of it as learning to walk before you can run. With perspective on where the web has been, you'll be better able to create the next big thing! If nothing else, you can use your knowledge to impress. Nothing shows dedication and real interest in a career like knowing and understanding its history.

MODERN-DAY WEBSITE DESIGN: DESIGNING FOR MANY SCREENS

Website design borrows from the basic principles of all effective designs, and adapts these techniques for the unique environment of the screen. Today, that screen might be a 20-inch (51 centimeter) laptop, or increasingly, a 4-inch (10 cm) smartphone or 9-inch (23 cm) tablet screen. Responsive design is the newest trend, and that means you design two or more website variations, depending on how users visit the site.

Size constraints have ramifications on design in many ways. It's not just about text size. How do you provide great graphics in the tiny real estate of a smartphone screen? Are buttons the best way to provide navigational features, or is there a better way when you're limited by size, such as swiping or tilting? These are questions that you need to answer as you adapt website designs for other, possibly smaller, platforms.

Responsive design involves designing various similar displays for website/smartphone/tablet/phablet.

Web designers learn how to apply basic design principles to their craft regardless of the site they are designing. They learn about and practice these design principles at school and/or on the job. A bachelor's (four-year) or associate's (two-year) degree in graphic design is best for entry-level positions, and about 300 colleges and art schools in the U.S. offer art and graphic design programs accredited by the National Association of Schools of Art and Design.

DESIGNING FOR MANY TYPES OF WEBSITES

In addition to knowing how to design for a number of different platforms, it's important that you understand the different genres of sites on the web today. Each has its own design approach and need. You'll likely find yourself designing for a number of different genres of sites, depending on the company you work with and its specialties.

Website Design Principles

The basic principles of great design involve creating a visual element, such as a website, that has harmony, balance, proportion, and hierarchy. It also must accurately and elegantly convey anything that is meant to be emphasized or understated.

A designer's knowledge of these principles informs all her decisions when designing a website. These include picking complimentary colors, determining which graphics to use and where, selecting typefaces, deciding on spacing and layout, considering the best size relationships between elements, incorporating whitespace (the space between words), and more. When you become a seasoned designer, you might even violate one of these principles on purpose to create a certain effect. For example, a site that purposely is out of balance can create a feeling of shock or discomfort, as well as produce a feeling of movement.

Designing a single website for one fixed-sized screen is a thing of the past. Your websites will need to respond to the visitor's device and adjust appropriately. The goal, of course, is to provide a beautiful and consistent experience, whether on a laptop, smartphone, tablet, or phablet, which are smartphone-tablet hybrids.

When it's all said and done, perhaps the most important question you can ask about a website's design is, "Is it easy to use?" Whether "use" means navigate, view, read, order from, or learn from is irrelevant. A savvy designer understands that a design must be easy to use and meet the viewers' needs.

If a neat or unique design gets in the way of conveying the message of the website, the designer has failed. Although it's important to be aware of the latest and greatest website design trends, the principles of good design and a positive user experience should always win out in the end.

The good news is that the basic principles of design mentioned here will lead you on your way to creating great websites. A website that incorporates, such principles as balance, harmony, and proportion is by definition easy to use and enjoy. These ancient ideas about design do indeed translate to the modern medium of websites.

Web designers can find job opportunities in a number of industries, including Internet service providers, Internet consulting firms, and web design companies. Advertising firms and graphic design shops also hire web designers. An increasing number of large companies maintain a staff of in-house designers. Finally, web designers with strong portfolios can establish careers as independent contractors, providing creative services to businesses or individual clients.

Sites that you might design for are likely to fit into one of the following genres:

- **Commerce sites** enable viewers to purchase products and/or services. For example, major design considerations for the Amazon.com website include responsiveness to media used; ease-of-use; consistent and recognizable approach to scrolling, scanning, and searching; brand recognition; proper and secure use of purchasing processes; and general reliability and security. If you're specializing in commerce sites, you'll want to become familiar with "shopping cart" website design programs, such as Magento, that specialize in creating e-commerce websites.

- **Brochure, or informational, sites** provide valuable information to their visitors. Wikipedia is a popular one, but also in this category are governmental sites, educational forums, and even certain company sites. When your main goal is to provide information, design considerations center on how text and graphics are presented in the best and quickest way possible. Some of these sites also have stores where visitors can purchase products, so they could also be considered commerce sites.

- **Database/catalog-driven sites** provide visitors with access to a large body of data, typically showcasing products that can be purchased. The best of these types of sites are easy to use and understand, are interactive and responsive, and use a design that is relevant and appropriate to the topic.

- **SaaS (Software as a Service) sites** provide "clouds" (networks of remote computers) where visitors go to access software, exchange data, etc. In essence, they provide web applications that users can access without having to download software. Often, the focus of building SaaS websites is more technical in nature—making sure that the programs are easy to access, secure, and load in most browsers, for example—rather than design-oriented. These sites are designed to be responsive, and easy to use and follow, with the user's needs in mind.

- **Blogs** are personal websites that users create to record and share frequent opinions, musings, stories/poems, and so on. Companies, organizations, and other affiliations also have blogs centered on their purpose and activities. Many blogs share similar designs, thus the more recent trend has been to specialize the look and feel of blogs to reflect the topics covered by its author. The challenge in that case is to create a unique blog with a specialized design that doesn't detract from its content.

- **Intranets** are local, restricted web-like sites, usually created and maintained by a company or organization for the purposes of communicating privately with its employees or members. The design challenges you'll have here are similar to any informational site, with the added constraint that such sites typically use specific fonts, colors, brands, and logos that identify the site as belonging to the organization.

Did you notice any patterns in this list? Regardless of the type of site, you need to be able to design something that is easy to use, meets the users' needs, and is fun and inviting to visit. That's easier said than done, and takes education and experience to get it right.

This list isn't meant to be exhaustive. Keep in mind that things change quickly on the Internet, so be sure you do more research before you begin to interview. You need to know what is "out there," so to speak, and have a basic understanding of the newest trends. Before you interview with any company, you should spend at least an hour on the web learning all about them. Spend time on their site, but also on sites created using various designs. Google, in this instance, is your best friend.

AN ON-THE-JOB SCENARIO

Did you know that people who visualize success are more likely to achieve it? With that in mind, picture yourself in a few years. You've just graduated from college with a degree in graphic design and, after some job searching and living at home for a while, you've landed your first job at Creative People Corp., a (fictitious) graphic design firm specializing in creating functional and attractive websites and blogs for its clients.

" "

It is our choices, Harry, far more than our abilities, that show what we truly are.

PROFESSOR DUMBLEDORE

It's a good thing you interned with a graphic designer during college, because you are already familiar with creating logos and icons, and using **typography** appropriately. You also became familiar with **Adobe Photoshop** and **Adobe Illustrator**, which are used to create and edit photos, art, and illustrations, as well as with **Adobe InDesign**, which is used to create layouts. It's because of your familiarity and comfort with these products and technologies (and your great personality) that you landed this entry-level position. Of course, you realize that hot technologies come and go, and you're committed to (and enjoy keeping up with) the latest cool trends and programs.

At Creative People Corp., you'll be working with and for the senior designer, who explains to you the overall concept of a website the company is developing for a new client. The senior designer determines the vision for the site (based on the client's wishes), and it's your job as part of the team to make it happen. With that goal in mind, you'll produce graphic sketches, designs, and copy layouts for online content. You'll determine the size and arrangement of graphic material and copy, select the style and size of type, and arrange the layout based upon available space, knowledge of layout principles, and aesthetic design concepts.

It's your job as part of the team to interpret the client's vision into a functional and effective website. The senior designer helps to translate the client's needs and desires into a great user experience. Your job is the hands-on process of making that happen.

As part of that process, you'll either create or be given logos and graphics for use on the site. If you are tasked to create them, you'll do that in a program such as Adobe Illustrator. When you need to edit or enhance photos, you'll use a program such as Adobe Photoshop.

To bring all the elements together and manage them effectively, you'll use a **content management system (CMS)**, a program used to manage the content of your website. A CMS enables designers to create and edit their websites without needing a **webmaster**.

The following are four of the most popular:

- **WordPress** is a free and open source blogging tool and a content management system based on PHP, a scripting language. It runs on a web hosting service and has a plug-in architecture and a template system. It's known as being very easy to set up and customize. WordPress is used by more than 18.9 percent of the top 10 million websites as of August 2013. WordPress is also the most popular blogging system in use on the web, at more than 60 million websites, as reported in *Forbes* magazine.

- **Joomla!** is another free and open source CMS based on **PHP**. It's known for its powerful extensions, and for how well it manages different user permissions. According to the *Joomla! Community Magazine*, Joomla! has been downloaded more than 35 million times.

- **Dreamweaver**, part of Adobe's CS6 offering, is an industry standard web development tool. Dreamweaver enables programmers to build complex interactive websites using HTML and JavaScript. Although its full version is about $400, you can download trial versions for free. Adobe offers a Dreamweaver-related certification that validates to potential employers your entry-level skills in web communication.

- **Drupal**, also free and open source, is another great example of a CMS. Keep in mind that by the time you read this, there will be newer products out there. Your employer will likely determine and provide the tools you'll use to do your job, and you'll get lots of on-the-job training on how to use them. That said, it's a good idea to be aware of the various tools available, even if you don't end up using all of them.

CONTRACTING YOUR SKILLS TO VARIOUS CLIENTS

Although the scenario discussed in the last section is more likely how most web designers start off—working for a web design firm or

The PHP Scripting Language and Open-Source Software

You can't really get away with discussing how website designers do their jobs these days without mentioning *PHP*, a free server-side scripting language designed for web development released under the PHP License. PHP is installed on more than 244 million websites and on 2.1 million web servers. At one time the initials stood for Personal Home Page, but PHP now stands for "PHP: Hypertext Preprocessor." PHP commands can be embedded directly into an HTML source document. It has also evolved to include a command-line interface, which is a type of human—computer interface that relies solely on textual input and output, and can be used in standalone graphical applications. Many larger enterprise sites use PHP directly, rather than a CMS program such as the ones described previously.

Open source is a term you'll be hearing a lot, if you haven't already. Open source software is software that can be freely used, changed, and shared by anyone and was created under the Open Source License. Open source software is often developed in a collaborative manner. The Open Source Initiative (OSI) maintains and regulates the definition of open-source software and its licenses. The OSI is a nonprofit corporation that advocates for the benefits of open source and builds bridges among different constituencies in the open source community. What this means for you is access to free, well-built software programs such as WordPress, Drupal, and Joomla!, to name a few.

other larger company "in house" as part of a team—there are many designers these days who work as freelancers, also referred to as contract-based employees. In fact, the U.S. Bureau of Labor Statistics reports that about a quarter of web developers are self-employed.

They might be assigned to a particular client's project and work on that project only. They are paid, usually a lump sum, for completion of that particular website. Once that project is finished their contract ends, although the company may hire them again for another project. The disadvantages to such an arrangement are that contract workers typically don't have company benefits such as health insurance, and, of course, they don't have the stability and reliability of a full-time job. Also, they have to arrange to pay their own income taxes. However, they do often have much more flexible work hours and expectations, and they are generally free to work for other companies.

Don't close yourself off to accepting a contract position. Even though it's not a full-time job, it's experience, which is what you need and probably lack at this stage in considering your career. Plus, you never know. If you do a great job and show that you're a team player, you very well may be offered a full-time job at some later point.

PREPARING FOR A CAREER IN WEB DESIGN

If it's important, it bears repeating, right? Remember, the web is constantly changing. Regardless of the latest and greatest technology that currently defines the web, it will be replaced by something even better and faster—soon. The web doesn't stand still and nothing is set in stone. That's one of the great things about the web. It is constantly evolving.

The web doesn't and won't stay in its current format, but that doesn't mean you shouldn't learn how to use the current technologies and approaches to web design. Learning all about CSS, JavaScript, and WordPress, as well as being well-versed in Photoshop and Illustrator, for example, will give you a solid foundation, and it will allow you to "talk the talk" with other

> ## " "
> ## *To improve is to change, so to be perfect is to change often.*
> ### WINSTON CHURCHILL

designers. With a solid foundation of the current technologies, you can more easily step forward into whatever cool thing exists on the horizon for web design.

You can't possibly know all there is to know about website design when you interview, and employers don't expect their entry-level employees to be experts. What you want to convey is that you have a real enthusiasm for the field, a willingness to learn, and some aptitude for the work.

By the same token, there is much you can do to prepare for a career in web design. You do need to get some experience, whether it's on campus or through an internship. This is one field where having hands-on experience is a must. You might even be able to gain that important hands-on experience in your school's media lab, or even on your own, at home on your laptop. Most of the programs that you'll use to start out are free thanks to open source, and you can simply search for "CSS tutorial" or "HTML tutorial" on the web and find many high-quality, step-by-step, hands-on video tutorials. Don't be afraid to get out there and create some websites. The barrier to learning is low and inexpensive. Perhaps the most important first step is to get an education that prepares you for the job.

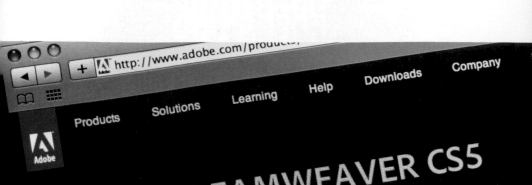

What is Dreamweaver?

Design, develop, and maintain standards-based web

Adobe® Dreamweaver® CS5 software empowers designers and d
websites with confidence. Design visually or directly in code, dev
systems, and accurately test browser compatibility thanks to inte
new Adobe CS Live online service.* CS Live services are compl

You need a working knowledge of programs like
Adobe Dreamweaver to succeed in website design.

2 PREPARING FOR A CAREER IN WEBSITE DESIGN

A re you interested in and excited by the idea of creating designs and interfaces that users love to use and visit? Are you unafraid of learning new technologies? Do you enjoy constant change and want to be on the cusp of what's new and exciting on the Internet? Do you get excited by the challenge of figuring out what the audience wants and needs, and want to learn how to translate those needs to a design? Do you believe you have some degree of artistic talent, creativity, and imagination? If you answered yes to any of these questions, then website design is a good career for you.

Since you've picked up this book, you probably already have some idea that a career in web design is for you. This chapter covers the educational background and skill set you need to get started in the field. Before you get started, keep in mind one of this chapter's main takeaways: *Get practice and experience building and creating websites wherever you can*. Experience, even if it's simply creating and designing your own websites on your home laptop, will help get your foot in the door. Your goal should be to start building a portfolio right away.

The good news is that career opportunities for web designers are expected to grow 22 percent from 2010 to 2020, according to the U.S. Bureau of Labor Statistics. Demand will be driven by the growing popularity of mobile devices and e-commerce. Web design is a career that's here to stay—and only shows promise of growth in the future.

PURSUING THE RIGHT KIND OF EDUCATION

You'll typically need either a four-year bachelor's degree or a two-year associate's degree in either a computer-related field such as computer science or information technology or in graphic design to have the best chances for securing an entry-level position in website design and development. There isn't usually one specific degree that website designers pursue. In fact, many degree programs can lead to website design employment, including computer science, graphic design, multimedia, web design, and marketing.

Although it's potentially trickier, you may be able to snag a web developer position even without those credentials if you have technical skills and practical experience. It seems as if you can ask three different sources and receive three different replies as to what you really do need in the way of formal education. According to the Bureau of Labor Statistics, for example, educational requirements for web designers vary tremendously. Requirements range from a high school diploma to a bachelor's degree, depending on the setting you work in and the type of design you do. However, to increase your chances of getting your foot in the door, and for better advancement once you're there, it's best to have a degree.

An associate's degree may be sufficient for designers who do not do a lot of programming. Some employers prefer web designers who have a computer degree and have taken classes

> " "
>
> *A piece of paper [a diploma] does not put you on a pedestal. It boils down to the quality of work you are capable of producing, where experience plays a monumental role. Degrees are a way to get your foot in the door, but your portfolio will be what helps you get all the way in.*

SAM DUNN,
CEO AND FOUNDER OF
ONE MIGHTY ROAR

in graphic design, especially when those designers are heavily involved in the website's visual appearance.

So what should you do? With so much ambiguity in the field, you can tailor your education experience to match your strengths and weaknesses. There is no one clear educational path to walk. Which way you go depends greatly on your personal circumstances, means, and goals. Remember that getting some hands-on experience and building your portfolio is your primary goal, no matter which educational path you pursue.

BACHELOR'S DEGREE VERSUS ASSOCIATE'S DEGREE

Deciding between a bachelor's degree and an associate's degree is a matter of figuring out what you want and need from your higher education experience. The first important step is to determine how much you can afford. More graduates than ever are leaving college with tens of thousands of dollars in student loans and no job to pay them off. If money is an issue, which it is for nearly all of us, it's smart to do a cost-benefit analysis of two-year versus four-year programs. Not only are two-year programs less expensive, you will also be out in the "real" world more quickly with the potential to earn a salary.

A recent CollegeMeasures.org report that analyzed wage statistics in Virginia found that in many industries, graduates with associate's degrees earned only slightly less their first year on the job than bachelor's degree graduates. Considering that the cost of a two-year, in-state college is conservatively around $45,000, it may be worth your while to consider an associate program specific to web or graphic design. Although this report did not single out web design jobs, it's a trend that's worth watching.

An associate's degree typically allows you more hands-on computer skills and teaches less about art theory. A four-year degree will give you those hands-on computer skills, but will also help more with the "soft" skills, such as art and design. There are other aspects of a four-year degree that set you apart as well. Although many of the things you learn with a four-year degree might not translate directly to your day-to-day job duties, you will be learning invaluable, important life lessons and strategies that just make you a better person, and therefore a better employee. These include becoming more organized, less selfish, more open-minded, more knowledgeable about the world in general, getting perspective on your views and outlook, building skills in rhetoric and persuasion, learning how to work with people who are different from you, and becoming more independent. These are "soft" traits that you will theoretically develop as you age and mature regardless, but immersion in college jump-starts and accelerates this growth. In addition, college can be an incubation place for creativity, and your future business partner might be living in your dorm.

Having a four-year degree is probably going to make you more marketable when you're looking for that first job. However, that's true only when you have a portfolio as impressive and developed as the person with the associate's degree. Your portfolio will set you apart, regardless of your degree type. The more on-the-job experience you acquire, the less your degree will matter to potential employers.

CHOOSING A SCHOOL AND A MAJOR

There are about 300 U.S. colleges and art schools that offer art and graphic design programs accredited by the National Association of Schools of Art and Design. Even more schools offer degrees in computer science and information technology, and these are all suitable stepping-stones into web design. You can even take classes online. Search for "graphic design program" and "web design program" to get started. However, before you sign up and give anyone your money, make sure you evaluate the program carefully to make sure it's legitimate. Help from a parent and guidance counselor might be wise here. It's easy to get scammed if you're not savvy about your investments.

Be sure to pick a degree that's relevant to your pursuits. If you are considering the pros and cons of different majors, think about the areas in which your skills are lacking and find something that complements your talents, whether it's computer science, multimedia, web design, marketing, or another field.

Regardless of the school and major you choose, you need to make the best of your educational experience by combining it with opportunities to build your portfolio. Use your university to make connections and find internships. Meet and work with other like-minded students in order to make connections that will last. Also, enter design contests as they are offered on your campus. Free press and accolades are great résumé- and portfolio-boosters.

THE LAST WORD: ATTEND COLLEGE OR NOT?

If you're still debating whether you should pursue a degree at all, research and answer these questions:

- How would a degree improve your current skill set?
- Do you need the structure that school provides to keep yourself motivated and on track?
- Would being in school hinder your pursuit of real-life experience, or open doors for it?
- How do you compare to the designers who have the jobs that you want?

Although a degree isn't for everyone, it can be a great path to get where you want to go, especially when you pair it with real-life experience. Many large companies won't even look at your portfolio and résumé unless you have some type of accredited degree. It helps get you an interview.

GETTING CERTIFICATIONS

Web developers can also take courses to get certifications, including Certified Web Developer, Certified Internet Webmaster, and Advanced Web Developer, all of which demonstrate varying levels of expertise. If you really want to be on the cutting edge, consider getting a certificate in Mobile Application Development. There is also a movement in the United States to create a web design certification. Countries such as Canada and Switzerland have already established successful design certifications.

Other certifications come from established companies in the industry. For example, Adobe offers a Dreamweaver-related certification that validates to potential employers you have entry-level skills in web communication. Many of these types of certifications aren't expected or required for entry-level positions. In fact, you might find that your employer offers to pay for your certifications after you've been on the job a while.

A college degree is almost always a great first step to success in any technical field.

The bottom line is this: experience is always more important than certifications. Your best approach is to highlight your knowledge by building a portfolio that showcases your experience. The good news is that you can start learning many of the skills you need with free, **open source programs** and a little bit of pluck. The next section covers the skill set you need to develop as you get that experience.

BUILDING A MARKETABLE SKILL SET

Web designers need to have coding skills using such languages as HTML, CSS, PHP, and JavaScript. As you learn and practice, you should be building a portfolio that showcases your knowledge

of these languages, as well as your creative application of them in the form of great designs. This section discusses the basic technologies you need to learn and use and gives you some places to start your education.

Note the order of the sections here. This is the order in which you should learn about these technologies. Get a good working knowledge of HTML before you move on to CSS. After you are comfortable using CSS, you're ready to move on to JavaScript, and so on.

LEARNING TO USE HTML

As you have already read, HTML is the markup language that allows designers to code text and graphics with certain tags so that they appear with certain characteristics and styling.

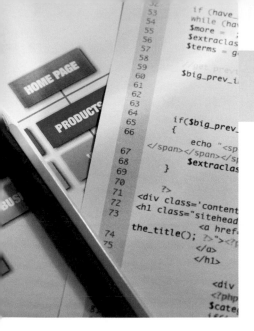

It's the basic language used on the web to convey text and graphics. The current standard is HTML5. In addition to developing a solid understanding of HTML tags and knowing how and when to use them, be sure that you're aware of the newest developments and updates to HTML5, and so on.

There are great tutorials on the web for learning how to use HTML, most of which include hands-on exercises and steps that you follow to build a sample page. Simply search Google for "HTML tutorial." Two good places to start are w3schools.com and codecademy.com.

LEARNING TO USE CSS

CSS provides a way to consistently style websites and to separate the content and the styling of a website. Style sheets are more efficient than just using HTML because they enable many pages to share formatting aspects and allow for repetitive structural content. The current version is CSS3, and you should be familiar with its improvements and updates. To get started, simply search Google for "CSS tutorial," or start with the websites mentioned in the previous section.

LEARNING TO USE JAVASCRIPT

JavaScript is the scripting language, often referred to as a client-side scripting language, that tells the user's browser how a website should appear and function. It's good for things such as validating forms, showing or hiding elements dynamically, creating animations, and communicating with the server in the

```
<script language="javascript">
    Event.observe(window, 'load', init, false)
    function init() {
        Lightbox.init();
    }

</script>

<script language="javascript">
function sprawdz_add_product(this){
    _(false);        _dd customer(this){
```

background. The JavaScript you write can be viewed by anybody visiting your site, and is therefore not a good place for security-sensitive elements such as **CAPTCHA** verification, where you re-enter the squiggly letters or numbers you see into a box to verify that you're a real human, and passwords. JavaScript powers some interactive web animations, too, such as games and fields. A great hands-on and interactive beginner JavaScript tutorial can be found at w3schools.com.

LEARNING TO USE PHP

PHP is a free "server-side" scripting language designed for web development. When someone visiting your site accesses a PHP file, the PHP is executed on the server and its output is sent back to the user. PHP is usually used in combination with a database to store and edit user and site data. It's better for sensitive data, and it doesn't rely on the user having JavaScript. Search for "PHP tutorial" or visit one of the previously mentioned sites to get started.

LEARNING TO USE SPECIFIC PROGRAMS SUCH AS WORDPRESS OR DREAMWEAVER

Recall that WordPress (wordpress.org), Drupal (drupal.org), and Joomla! (joomla.org) are free and open source content management systems (CMSs) based on PHP. A content management system is basically a program that enables you to publish, edit, and modify content from a central interface, typically in a collaborative environment, where multiple editors and authors can make changes to one document.

These programs are known for being very easy to set up and customize. Especially because they are free, your next step after becoming comfortable with the technologies above is to download one of these programs and start creating pages. It's better to build a foundation of knowledge at least about HTML and CSS before you start using one of these CMSs. Having knowledge of how CMSs work, and having a working knowledge of one of these programs in particular, is important. The one selected is up to you. It might be smart to ask fellow website designers or teachers in your area what they are using. When you run into questions, it would be nice to have a personal contact from whom you can solicit help, although you can also find answers from web development communities on the Internet.

If you want to learn to use a program such as **Adobe Dreamweaver**, which currently costs about $400, you can download a free trial version. There are also price-reduced versions marketed especially for students that cost about $100. There are also cloud-based solutions that also save you money. To download the student-discounted versions, Adobe simply requires that you be at least thirteen years of age and be enrolled in an accredited school, be it a university, college, or secondary school. Homeschoolers can also qualify as long as their schooling meets their state regulations. For more information about Adobe's student discount program, visit adobe.com/education/students.

Rock Stars in the Industry

As part of educating yourself about the industry, it's smart to be aware of and follow leaders and trendsetters. The point of following people who are successful in the industry is that, along with learning about and gaining exposure to the hottest web design trends and approaches, you'll learn how successful people present themselves out in the web design world. You can emulate their behaviors, learn from their designs, and forge your own path to success. This sidebar highlights just a handful of the movers and shakers. Don't be afraid to go online and find designs and approaches that speak to you personally, and follow the people behind them as well.

- **Vitaly Friedman** is one of the founders and editor-in-chief of the popular *Smashing Magazine* (smashingmagazine.com), which is a cutting-edge, beautiful, and functional web design blog. A self-described writer, speaker, and author, Friedman says that he "loves beautiful content."

- **Cameron Moll** is a designer, speaker, and author living in Sarasota, Florida, with his wife and four sons. He's the founder of Authentic Jobs Inc., among other ventures (authenticjobs.com). Check out his website at cameronmoll.com.

- **Jakob Nielsen** is sometimes called "the king of usability" and "the smartest person on the web." Nielsen's web

Jakob Nielsen

designs can be seen at nngroup.com. You can subscribe to receive his weekly Alertbox articles about interface usability and website design at nngroup.com/articles/subscribe.

- **Veerle Pieters** began her career in 1992, when she became a freelance designer under the name of Duoh! She founded the website duoh.com in 2000. Pieters's design blog (veerle.duoh.com) is well known and cited, and her designs are distinctive and inspirational.

- **Dave Shea** is the owner of the design studio Bright Creative (brightcreative.com). Shea has a very uplifting portfolio and loves icon design. He has many ongoing projects, including Zen Garden (csszengarden.com), as well as his personal web blog at mezzoblue.com.

These are just a few of the industry's rock stars out there, creating great designs on the web. Be sure to do your "homework" and find ones that speak to your style and approach. As a start, bookmark and visit smashingmagazine.com, which keeps its finger on the pulse of the web design industry.

Unless you have a compelling reason to start with Dreamweaver or another consumer-based product, it's smarter to start your educational journey with the free products. They will get you where you need to go just as effectively.

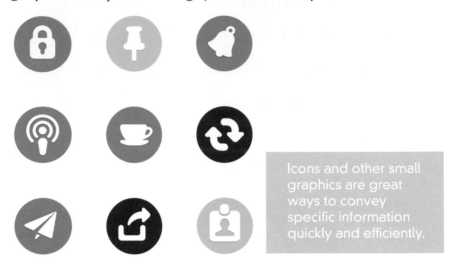

Icons and other small graphics are great ways to convey specific information quickly and efficiently.

LEARNING TO CREATE GRAPHICS AND ICONS

Learning to create graphics and icons on your own can be a bit trickier. Although there are many great tutorials online, you'll almost always need a program such as Adobe Illustrator or Adobe Photoshop, both of which are quite expensive. Of course, you probably qualify for Adobe's discounted student program mentioned previously.

If you don't have cheap or easy access to the Adobe line of products, a better first step is to play around with free alternatives such as GIMP, Pixlr, Scribus, and Inkscape. They can all help you learn the graphic design ropes until you're able to purchase the Adobe products. These products provide a canvas for you to hone and develop your design skills, which is likely what you're most lacking at this stage.

If you are new to design in general, or new to creating graphic design elements, it would be smart to take a graphic design class. Learning in a creative environment where you're given

Website Design

> **"** **"**
>
> *If you're already a student at a university and have no outside experience, it may be difficult to pursue a career in design.*
> *I say this only because personal friends of mine have struggled to find jobs in this current economic climate. Experience and something to show for your knowledge goes a long way.*

—DAVE LEGGETT, WEB DESIGNER

some direction and guidance, but allowed some freedom to develop your own vision, is a great way to hone these kinds of skills. Check your local community college or college branches for "introduction to graphic design" classes. If you've decided on a two- or four-year college route, make sure that graphic design classes are included in the program.

LEARNING TO SUCCEED

If you take only one thing away from reading this chapter, let it be this: The key to setting yourself apart in a job interview is a successful blend of education and experience. Add to your portfolio every chance you get. This should sound like a fun prospect to you. However, if the thought of building websites for the sake of building your portfolio makes you groan, you probably shouldn't be in this industry. You need to have a passion for the work. Having a passion for your job will make it so much more fun, and potential employers will pick up on your enthusiasm. Passion also leads to creativity.

Your experience will also give you a solid foundation as to the challenges and goals of web design, and it will allow you to

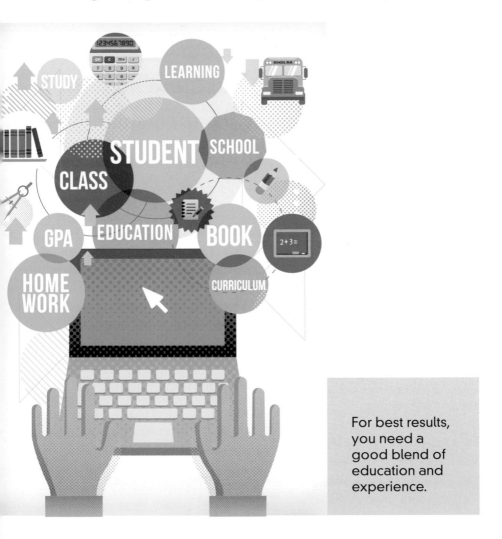

For best results, you need a good blend of education and experience.

> # " "
> ## *The most important thing is 'practice, practice, practice.' To improve the quality of your work, you have to keep pushing yourself further and further.*
>
> —WOLFGANG BARTELME, WEB DESIGNER

"talk the talk" with potential employers. With a firm understanding of the current technologies and experience in applying them, you can more easily adapt to the next cool program or approach that appears on the horizon.

Throughout your career, you also must keep up to date on new tools and computer languages. If you have a real passion for web design, this will happen naturally, as long as you keep an open mind and actively pursue new venues. Education is a lifelong pursuit. It doesn't stop after you graduate. In fact, you'll likely learn far more about web design on the job than you ever will in the classroom. With this in mind, you might wonder what the day-to-day job really looks like. Read on to find out!

How to Build Your Portfolio

By now you likely understand that having a portfolio is an important part of pursuing a career in web design, and it's never too early to start building one. Even without a "real" full-time job there are lots of creative ways to build a portfolio that showcases your work. Here are a few suggestions to get you started.

- **Create your own personal website.** If you want to be a website designer, you should definitely have your own website, or perhaps even several sites that have different themes and topics. Try to design each one around something interesting you've done, or something unique about you. If you're a long-distance runner on your school team, design one website as an homage to running. If you took a fantastic trip to the Caribbean last summer, give another site a tropical theme. You should continually adapt and improve your websites. Don't let them get stale. In addition to a home page, be sure to showcase custom 404 pages (a broken link page), contact forms, and any customized forms you've built.
- **Take a website design class and add that work to your portfolio.** If your local school doesn't offer classes or training, check out the nearest community college offerings. Pages you build in the classroom are fair game for your portfolio.
- **Create pages for imaginary clients.** Create "non-live" pages specific to local organizations that you know something about, bands you like, or even about your school or neighborhood. You should pick something you are knowledgeable about. As long as you make it clear to your

prospective employers that these are samples and not live designs, there is nothing wrong with honing your skills and improving your portfolio with these types of projects.

- **Find a free web template and modify it.** There are thousands of free templates on the web. Using an existing template to get an idea flowing is a great portfolio idea. Use a wireframe, or skeletal template, and add your own color schemes, themes, iconography, and style. You need to modify the template to the point where it is clearly your own design, and also credit the original wireframe template as your starting point.

Regardless of the methods you use, you should be continuously updating your portfolio with new and improved designs. As you gain experience, your portfolio will get better. Also, continually updating your pages shows that you're actively working to hone your web design skills.

Website design often requires employees to work together on projects and ideas.

Website Design

3 A DAY IN THE LIFE OF A WEBSITE DESIGNER

W hen companies create websites, it's a multi-step process, and the web designers are involved during every step. In this chapter, the day-to-day experiences you'll have when you are employed as a website designer are discussed. It compares and contrasts that same job in different settings, such as working for a large design firm, working in the design department of a large tech company, working for a smaller design company or nonprofit, and even working for yourself as a contractor. It also describes and outlines the basic job duties you'll have, regardless of the organization you work for.

All of the different variations of website design have their benefits and drawbacks, and it's smart to understand them so you can find your best fit based on your personality, strengths, and goals.

At this point, let's pretend that you've taken all the advice from the previous chapters to heart. You have the education and experience you need, have built a rocking portfolio, and have positioned yourself in the market well. Your next step is to find the right environment to showcase your skills and work toward your goals—that is, once you have identified them.

BEFORE YOU PUT YOURSELF OUT THERE

Before you start looking for a good professional fit, it's important that you take some time to evaluate and understand your career goals, personality traits, and needs. Although you might not find the perfect job that fits all your characteristics, it's still a valuable and important process to go through. If nothing else, knowing what you want and who you are will come across in an interview, and can very likely set you apart from many other candidates. It conveys confidence and shows the interviewer that you have thought about your career and the "big picture," so to speak.

The questions that follow are a good place to start. You might not be able to answer them all right now. Some of the answers will only become clear as you gain experience, take classes, and build your portfolio. The answers you give will also undoubtedly change as you grow and change. It's therefore important to revisit these questions as you gain experience, knowledge, perspective, and years.

Keep in mind that there are no wrong answers, and it's vitally important that you answer honestly and realistically.

- What are your career goals? Do you want to become an expert in a certain industry? Do you want to work for the best-known web development company out there or be the "boss" in five years? Is your plan to learn as much as you can about website design, or to learn enough so you can some day start your own company? Do you want to build a career that gives you flexible hours and complements your busy life? Are you using website design as a jumping-off point into a different career? Think about what you want from your job and career, and be honest.

- Do you feel comfortable taking on a project with very little guidance and few guidelines, or are you more likely to succeed when you have solid guidelines and procedures for completing a project?

- How likely are you to press your ideas upon others in a group when you think they're good ones? Do you think it's better to keep quiet at first and make sure you understand all the variables, or are you more likely to jump in with your ideas and make them known?

- Do you feel comfortable in risky situations, ones that might jeopardize your standing but might also have great payoffs? Or are you more successful and comfortable in less risky settings?

- Does direct competition with others bring out your best efforts, or are you more likely to shut down when you feel an environment is too competitive and not collaborative?

- Do you enjoy "sweating the details," or are you more motivated by the "big picture" of any project?

- If you had to pick only one path, would you rather become an expert in only one particular area, or be somewhat well versed in many areas of your profession?

- Do you enjoy brainstorming different and new ways to solve problems or reach goals, or do you feel better going with the established methods?

This is just a sampling of the questions on career aptitude tests. The point is to measure certain personality characteristics and match them to careers that complement those traits. If you are still struggling with finding the best career for you, check out the more complete test you can take online, such as the *Psychology Today* online test at psychologytoday.tests.psychtests.com.

Determining the mission, or purpose, of a website is an important first step.

THE BASIC JOB DESCRIPTION

Hopefully, you now have some idea of your career goals and a realistic understanding of your strengths and weaknesses. This section sets the groundwork for the basic job duties you'll have as a website designer and developer. The tasks and responsibilities listed here are all-inclusive. This means you won't likely be responsible for all these aspects of design, particularly if you work for a large company, where job titles are more strictly defined.

A web designer and developer is typically responsible for the design, layout, and coding of a website, blog, intranet, and so on. You'll be involved with the technical and graphical aspects of a website, which means how the site works and how it looks. You might also be involved with the maintenance and update of an existing site.

In order to design a website, you have to:

- Establish the purpose of the website based on the target audience. Is its purpose to sell a product or service, or is it simply informational? Does it serve the company employees only, or is it open to the entire web? Determining the target audience is a very important part of establishing the purpose of the site, because the demographics of that audience will greatly influence the design approach you take.

- Identify the type of content the site will host. Recall the main types of websites. There are e-commerce sites, such as Amazon, which enable viewers to purchase products or services; brochure or informational sites, such as Wikipedia, which provide information to their visitors; database/catalog sites, which provide access to a large amount of data in an easy-to-access way; SaaS sites, which provide access to software and data in the cloud; blogs, which are diary-type websites where bloggers write and record thoughts and musings on a regular basis; and intranets, which are local, restricted, web-like sites, usually created and maintained by an organization for the purpose of communicating privately with its employees or members.

If you're designing a blog, it should have a different look than, say, an e-commerce site.

- Determine the functionality that the site must support. For example, will it handle forms, financial transactions, or interactive components? The purpose of the site and the type of content you'll be providing largely determine the functionality you'll need to provide.

- Provide guidance about layout, colors, and styles. These decisions may be influenced by corporate guidelines that determine the look and feel of all the company's websites, blogs, and intranets.

The answers to these points determine the type of technology you'll use and how complex the site will be. After these guidelines are established and agreed upon, you'll then need to do the following:

- Write the programming code, either from scratch or by adapting existing website software—for example, CMSs such as Dreamweaver or Joomla!—and graphics packages, such as Adobe Photoshop and Illustrator, to meet the website's requirements.

- Test the website and identify any technical problems. Your IT (information technology) group may get involved at this point, or your group may be responsible for having these technical skills.

- Upload the site onto a server and register it with different search engines. Knowledge of search engine optimization may be part of your job requirements, or this might be part of the IT department's job, or an entirely different department, depending on the size of the company for which you work.

As you read these bullet points, note the job descriptions that get you excited as well as those that don't. This process is part of discovering your passion. Although you might not be able to do it all at once, you need to know where your passion lies and acquire skills in those areas.

Of course, how much you do of any of these tasks depends at

Website Design

least in part on the environment in which you work, and also on experience. Regardless of where you work you will usually be part of a team, which includes a web author, editor, and an account manager, at least. Regardless, the scope of the entry-level website designer position can vary greatly, depending on where you work.

THE ENTRY-LEVEL POSITION DEPENDS ON YOUR WORK SETTING

Do you recall from Chapter 1 the made-up scenario about Creative People Corp., the fictional design studio? Well, that's only one type of job setting that you might experience. There are many different types of job settings that you might find yourself working in as a web designer, and each one has its benefits and drawbacks. Remember, you're more likely to be successful and happy if you find a setting that matches your goals, needs, and personality traits. Keep in mind that these descriptions are generally true, and for every rule, there is an exception.

WORKING FOR A LARGE DESIGN FIRM

Larger companies, design and otherwise, tend to have solid defined job titles for each department and division. These jobs also are more likely to be highly specific and segmented to a particular task or skill. That means you'll come in at an entry-level position with a very defined job description, and you'll likely be closely managed and mentored by a senior designer, or someone in a similar position, who explains to you the overall concept of the website to which you'll be contributing. The overall concept, including the design, the look and feel, and probably even the types of graphics and icons you'll be tasked to create, will have already been decided upon. In a large corporate setting, you're much less likely to be in the position to pitch your own creative ideas or develop your own graphics for consideration.

Working for a large design firm means being comfortable designing for other people's visions.

The senior designer, or perhaps even her boss, determines the vision for the site based on the client's wishes, and it's your job as part of the team to make it happen. Your team will produce the graphic sketches, designs, and copy layouts based on the established guidelines. Your job, based on your experience and expertise, will focus on only one of these areas. For example, you might concentrate solely on creating certain icons meeting the design specifications in their various sizes, file types, and iterations.

The benefits of a job such as this are that you have established guidelines and a clear path to success. There is rarely any ambiguity in what your employer expects from you, or what you need to do to complete a project. You're more likely to have established guidelines and procedures for getting work done, as well as receive consistent and detailed training in using the software and programs you'll need, which are often the best and most recent versions out there.

In addition, your company is likely to pay for courses and certifications that will further your education. The perks in general, such as health club memberships, better health insurance, more liberal vacation policies, and more, are usually better at large companies. Generally speaking, job security is higher with larger companies, too. Also, it never hurts to have a well-known organization on your résumé, especially when you're starting out.

Perhaps the more important benefit is that you're surrounded by lots of smart people with more experience than you. You will learn a lot in this type of environment, which has been fine-tuned, in theory, by many people's years of experience and knowledge.

The drawbacks are probably evident by now. There is potentially a certain amount of monotony in these jobs, and you're not always rewarded for thinking in new and creative ways. The "status quo" more often rules the day. Your job will be very specific to one or a few certain tasks, so you need to be able to thrive in that environment. If you are more risk-averse and feel more comfortable when given clear instructions for accomplishing a task, a large corporation can be a good fit.

WORKING IN THE DESIGN DEPARTMENT OF A LARGE COMPANY

The experience of working in the design department within a large company is, in many ways, similar to working for a large design firm. The exception is that perhaps the role of design might not be as important and central in a large company whose bottom line is driven by some other product or service. Design becomes a practical endeavor, and it's only helpful as long as it contributes to the bottom line.

In this setting, your job will be to design and maintain the websites, blogs, intranets, and the like of the organization, which will no doubt have a very standard look and feel to them, based on corporate identity guidelines. For example, certain special text and buttons are always a shade of blue that matches the company's logo.

Again, the benefits of working for a large organization include established guidelines, consistent training, access to the latest and greatest software and programs, and the chance to rub elbows and learn from lots of other smart people. The disadvantages are similar, too, and one could argue that job security is not quite as solid in this setting, since your services don't contribute directly to the bottom line. Also, you have to be comfortable with the idea that website design is not as important to such organizations compared to working for a design firm.

WORKING FOR A SMALLER COMPANY OR NONPROFIT

Working for smaller design firms, tech companies, or nonprofits can be a great experience that will offer you exposure to all aspects of website building. It can also be frustrating, political, and stressful. Smaller firms tend to be more supportive, less bureaucratic, and more willing to hire workers embarking on new careers.

In a smaller setting, you are more likely to be able to get hands-on experience in many different aspects of website design, depending on your interests. You'll be exposed to a diverse range of activities and even get more involved in the day-to-day running of a business.

Smaller teams and a less regimented setting means that employees get to try their hand at various skills. They are more likely to be open to new ideas, more likely to take risks, and more likely to be collaborative. Your creative ideas are more likely to be considered and welcomed. You'll also more likely be working alongside senior employees, which provides great opportunities for learning from these seasoned professionals. This is particularly great for someone just starting out.

If you find yourself in the market and really want that big picture experience of doing a bit of everything related to web design, a smaller company is a better place to land. However, one of the biggest problems with many smaller organizations is that there can be a lot of office politics and nepotism, and this can create hostile and difficult work environments. Larger corporations tend to have strict policies about how people are hired and promoted, but they can still have their own brand of office politics.

Do your homework and research the office culture before you accept a position at a small firm. Find out if people are generally happy there, and why or why not. This is something you should do regardless of the company's size, but the impact of the culture at a smaller organization will be greater on your own job satisfaction.

The other drawbacks include fewer perks and less job stability. These companies just don't have the larger budgets of bigger organizations, which means you might not be able to further your education or get certifications until you've been there a while (or maybe not at all). Also, you might be using older software and devices.

If you are more comfortable taking risks, want to have a breadth of knowledge rather than a depth of one topic, want to contribute your ideas right away, or are more motivated by the "big picture" of any project, a smaller company or nonprofit is a better fit.

CONTRACTING YOUR SKILLS TO VARIOUS CLIENTS

As you read in Chapter 1, there are many designers who work as freelancers, or contract-based employees. Recall that the U.S. Bureau of Labor Statistics reported that about a quarter of web developers are self-employed. How does this look, and how likely are you to start a career in this manner?

Freelancing or contracting is typically something that only experienced designers do with any success. If you're just starting out, seeking contract work exclusively should be your last option. You will learn so much from working alongside other experienced designers. In fact, the amount you'll learn your first year on the job from others will astound you. You don't want to miss out on that learning experience.

Still, there's no harm in taking contract work as you look for a full-time job, or even doing contract work in addition to your job. Just make sure it doesn't violate any agreement you signed with your employer. Even if you didn't sign anything official, err on the side of caution. You shouldn't contract with a company who might in any way be a competitor or a client. And you should always do your contract work at home, during your personal time. Anything less could get you fired.

Why Choose a Nonprofit?

Nonprofit organizations are defined as corporations that attempt to fulfill a mission to improve the common good of society rather than to acquire and distribute profits. Examples of well-known and well-regarded nonprofits include National Public Radio (NPR), United Nation's International Children's Emergency Fund (UNICEF), the Smithsonian Institute, the Wikimedia Foundation, and Kiva.

If the thought of assimilating into the corporate culture makes your stomach turn, and you really want to make a difference in your career, you should consider employment at a nonprofit organization. Although nonprofits do typically pay less for the same positions across the board, there are many intangible benefits that can contribute to your quality of work. Also, statistics show that salary gap is narrowing as the nonprofit sector recognizes the need to attract and retain talent. In fact, it's not unheard of for large-nonprofit executives to earn six-figure salaries. Nonprofits also compensate in other ways by offering flextime, more vacation days, a relaxed dress code, and other non-monetary benefits. You're much more likely to contribute to a diverse range of activities and tasks. This is experience that can build your résumé and portfolio faster than other settings. Being involved in overlapping areas enables you to develop a range of transferable skills in a relatively short amount of time. Nonprofit experience also expands your networking potential. You'll be rubbing elbows with influential executives who work on their boards, donors and sponsors, government officials, and social activists, all of whom believe in the cause that you support. Perhaps the most inviting benefit is that you get to work toward a cause you care about, and make a living while doing it.

The Smithsonian Castle in Washington, D.C.

With contract work, the perks are basically nonexistent. Contract workers typically don't have company benefits such as health insurance, and are often expected to have access to the hardware and software needed to do the job.

Now that you know all the warnings and drawbacks about contract work, you might wonder when it would ever be a good idea. One great benefit of this approach is that it gets your foot in the door, and might very well lead to a full-time job. If you create a great product, you will get noticed. It's a less risky way for employers to "hire" someone, financially speaking. It might be your ticket in the door. The other benefit that many freelance designers enjoy is the flexible work hours. For this reason, many people with family obligations choose this route. Also, you're usually free to work for whomever you want, so your work may be more varied and interesting than if you worked for one company.

In any case, it's a great way to build your portfolio. Every contract job you get means experience, which is what you need and probably lack at this stage in your career. Besides, you

Regardless of company size, you will need good interpersonal skills.

> ❝ ❞
> *I choose my projects based on how well I connect with a company. I've worked on everything from ExpressionEngine 2.0's GUI to wonderful creative projects for the Library of Congress to sites for a wealth of small and large businesses.*
>
> —VEERLE PIETERS,
> FREELANCE GRAPHIC/WEB DESIGNER

never know. If you do a great job and show that you're a team player, you very well may be offered a full-time job.

SUCCESSFUL COMPANIES IN THE INDUSTRY

You can ask ten different web designers, or read ten different web design articles, and get ten different answers about leaders in this industry. The good news is that there are many great design agencies out there. The bad news is that companies come and go, and many don't survive. Those mentioned in this chapter were selected based in part on longevity and reputation, as well as geographic diversity. When visiting their websites, you can view samples of their work, see their current client lists, and, of course, view their online job postings.

- **The Creative Momentum (Atlanta, Georgia)** is a full-service design studio that has won numerous "best of" awards and targets custom web design and development. They specialize in custom web/interactive, SEO, custom graphic/logo design, branding, advertising, mobile design, and more. Check out their great designs at thecreativemomentum.com.

- **Perfect Search Design (Chicago, Illinois)**, founded in 2010, is a fast-growing organization that specializes in responsive design and development, SEO, social media, retargeting, and display advertising for their clients. They also have won numerous "best of" awards. Visit perfectsearchdesign.com.

- **Blue Fountain Media (New York, New York)** are a digital marketing agency focused on creative and results-driven solutions for companies ranging from start-ups to Fortune 1,000 companies. See bluefountainmedia.com.

- **Clikzy Creative (Washington, D.C.)** was recently rated the best website design company in Washington, D.C. This interactive website design agency and online marketing firm specializes in small- to medium-sized business in the areas of web design, online marketing, and e-commerce website design. Visit clikzy.com.

- **Forix Web Design (Portland, Oregon)**, started in 2007, and specializes in intuitive workflow apps for mobile platforms, effective and beautiful e-commerce systems, imaginative user experience sites, and award-winning designs. Check them out at forixwebdesign.com.

- **Isadora Design (Redondo Beach, California)** specializes in branding, web design and development, e-commerce sites, and responsive web design. Noted on several of the "best of" lists, the company acts as consultant, web designer, and developer all in one. Check them out at isadoradesign.com.

Of course, there are many great website design companies, and probably several located in your city. Do your own local searching as well. Start by visiting 10bestdesign.com/firms or topseos.com/rankings-of-best-web-design-companies for frequently updated lists of the best in the industry.

INCREASING YOUR ODDS OF SUCCESS

Regardless of where you end up working, there are certain skills and traits you should develop to increase your odds of success. To gain a favorable outcome in the working world of website design, you need to:

- Be adaptable and able to learn new techniques
- Have good interpersonal and communication skills
- Be able to work on your own or in a team
- Be able to work under tight deadlines
- Be able to multitask
- Be able to use your initiative

Recognize the areas where you naturally struggle, and make efforts to improve in them. Intrapersonal and communication skills in particular are critical in this field. If this isn't something that comes naturally to you, practice it. You can and should develop these skills over time. Having the best overall combination of skills and experience means no company would turn you down and you can earn top dollar.

Creating Mobile-Friendly Websites

You've read several times in this book how important it is as a website designer to keep up with the latest trends, technologies, and programs that affect your profession. One of the biggest trends right now is creating websites that work well in the desktop and laptop setting, but also port nicely to mobile devices. This is called responsive design, and you typically need to design two or more website variations, depending on how your users visit the site. Your mobile-friendly websites should adapt to the smaller size, certainly. But you also need to know how to incorporate various navigation techniques that are mobile- and finger-friendly, such as swiping or tilting; use colors and contrast that compliment the sunny settings people use their phone in, enable better onscreen keyboards for users, provide great graphics on the tiny smartphone screen, make sure the website loads quickly and professionally on a phone, and more. These are all issues that you need to address as you adapt website designs for other (smaller) platforms.

In response to the mobile revolution, new CSS tags have been developed to address many of these issues, and it would be smart for a website designer, aspiring or otherwise, to know how to use these styles. There is even a Mobile Application Development certification you can earn online through various universities. Just search for "Mobile Application Development certification" online. What is more important than being specifically well-versed in mobile-friendly sites, though, is the effort you put into being well-versed in the newest "big thing," and that you educate yourself about the latest and greatest website design trends. Your website design education will be a lifelong endeavor, and you need to be open and excited by that.

Responsive design means that your design will adjust and look great, no matter what kind of device it's viewed on.

Be sure you know the cost of living standards in the city where you'll work.

Website Design

4 BENEFITS AND SALARY

A t this point in the book, you should have a pretty good idea about the educational path you need to follow to become a website designer, including how important it is to get experience and build your portfolio whenever or wherever you can. You should also have a picture in your mind about what website designers do on the job, and how that job differs in various organizations and markets. Ultimately, you should have a feel for whether it's something that sounds interesting and exciting to you. If you've made it this far, you probably do think it's something you would like to do for a living. How that living is made and the typical salary and benefits earned by website designers across the United States are discussed in this chapter.

Keep in mind that, just like cost of living, salaries and, to a lesser degree, benefits, vary greatly across the United States. From coast to coast and big cities to smaller towns, it's vastly different. If you want to live and work on either coast, particularly in high-profile cities such as New York, Los Angeles, or San Francisco, your cost of living will average 30 to 40 percent more—your salary should generally reflect that. Conversely, you may not be offered as high a salary to work in a large Midwestern city or smaller town, but the cost of living there will be significantly less, Chicago excluded, which means your salary will be worth more, relatively.

Before you begin your job search, look closely at the areas in which you would like to live. For example, how much does it cost to rent an apartment in the desirable, fun area where people your age like to live? You'll need to have a realistic understanding of how far the salary offered will go. Before we get into the nitty-gritty details about money, though, let's discuss the other "intangibles"—the benefits and perks your company will offer to you as part of full-time employment.

WHAT YOU CAN EXPECT IN TERMS OF CORPORATE BENEFITS AND PERKS

The types, sizes, and amounts of benefits vary greatly across the board, but the good news is that companies in the tech field offer some of the most liberal and generous benefits available, and they typically cater to younger people. This means that these benefits are more likely to be things you'll enjoy receiving. As a reminder, you almost always have to be a full-time employee to enjoy a company's benefits. If you accept a part-time job or take on contract work, the company benefits aren't usually part of the package. Make sure you understand what is and isn't included when you accept a part-time or contract position.

Also, keep this general truism in mind: the larger the company, the better the benefits package. This is generally true because larger companies, as well as public sector government employers, have more money in their coffers—but there are exceptions to every rule. Many newer tech companies take an innovative approach to offering benefits as a way to attract talent, and you could very well find a smaller start-up with a great benefits package.

Health insurance is often offered to full-time employees.

BENEFITS YOU WILL MOST CERTAINLY RECEIVE

Benefits you will most certainly receive as a full-time employee in the Unites States include health insurance of some kind and a predetermined number of sick and vacation days. The amount, cost, and extent of these benefits can vary greatly.

According to the U.S. Bureau of Labor Statistics, the average number of annual paid holidays is ten. The average amount of vacation days is 9.4 after a year of service. If this is somewhere you see yourself staying for a while, consider not only the number of vacation days in the first year, but also how that number increases as you accumulate years in the company.

Almost half the medium and large employers surveyed by the U.S. Bureau of Labor Statistics offered either a defined benefit or a defined contribution pension plan, such as a 401K, where you save some of your earnings into a retirement account, and many employers will match the amount you put into retirement up to a certain percent. About 75 percent offer health insurance, but almost as many require employees to contribute toward the cost.

Note that smaller companies are much less likely to have contribution pension plans and to offer health insurance. As the kinks are ironed out of the Affordable Health Care Act, not having health insurance from your company may be less of a concern. However, you should be insured in one form or another. As a young person, you might not think that health insurance is important for you, but one car accident or injury could mean tens of thousands of dollars in medical expenses if you're not covered.

BENEFITS/PERKS YOU MAY BE OFFERED

Benefits/perks that are common in the high-tech fields and that you might have access to include paid educational programs and/or certifications, flextime and casual work environments, and special offerings such as gym memberships. Of these, the most valuable in terms of pure dollar benefit is the chance to further your education at the company's expense. Whether it's pursuing your master's degree or getting certified in Dreamweaver or some other website design technology, your educational efforts will make you more marketable and valuable at your current job, as well as down the line. Tuition reimbursement can largely benefit you in two ways: you save money by not having to pay for the classes, and you stand to earn more in the future because greater knowledge increases your value.

Of course, there may be "strings" attached, usually in the form of some employment agreement to stay at the company a certain amount of time after your education is complete. This is more likely to be the case when you're pursing a long-term degree such as a master's, rather than taking a series of classes to become certified in an area. Also keep in mind the word "reimbursement": you will likely need to pay for the classes initially, and only after you have completed the class and received a grade/rating deemed acceptable by your employer will you be reimbursed. Even with these conditions, it may well be worth it. As always, do your homework so you know what you're getting into.

> **Web design is an appealing career choice for artistic and creative people. It's seen as a potentially lucrative opportunity to be creative on a daily basis. But—beware— the competition is fierce.**
>
> CAMERON CHAPMAN, PROFESSIONAL WEB AND GRAPHIC DESIGNER

Especially in the fast-paced and ever-changing world of website design, it is critical that you keep up-to-date with trends and technologies. Having your company on board with this, monetarily and philosophically, is incredibly valuable.

In terms of the other perks and benefits, keep in mind that nearly all tech companies offer a casual dress code these days. They might tout it as something unique and special, but it is increasingly becoming the norm. Being able to set your own work schedule (flextime) or have the option to telecommute some days also falls under the "casual work environment" umbrella. It's up to you to decide how valuable these perks are and look for the ones that really matter. For example, if you work out on a regular basis, look for employers who offer gym memberships. Having paid

Bringing your pet to work might be a perk of the job.

access to a local gym is more of a norm these days, especially on the coasts, so this isn't asking too much.

ABOVE AND BEYOND: THE SPECIAL TOUCHES

Innovative companies have become increasingly creative in providing perks and benefits that will attract the types of employees they want. If you find a company boasting a culture that embraces your passions and interests, it's a win-win.

Benefits don't just stop at day care, flexible hours, and tuition reimbursement. Consider this long list of real perks that actual companies offer in today's market:

- Convenient services to make the other parts of your life hassle-free, such as on-site dry cleaning, concierge services, take-home meals, on-site meals delivered to your desk, and use of company vehicles.

- Bring your pet to work, every day!

Taking an Analytical Eye to Perks

One thing you might want to ask yourself is why a company might offer specific perks over others and what that says about the company's culture. For example, what might a company that offers such services as on-site dry cleaning, concierge services, allowing pets at work, and on-site meals delivered to your desk ultimately be getting from its employees? Could they perhaps be attempting to keep employees on-site for longer hours, or at least trying to make it as easy as possible for employees to spend more of their lives at work?

This is not to say you should be cynical of everything a company offers you. Perks are great, and they show that your employer values you and your needs. However, companies are in the business to make money and they have likely considered the costs versus the benefits of providing these perks. This is true with nonprofits also—any employer is going to attempt to get the most out of you for your salary.

If you're not jazzed by the idea of working extra long hours, for example, you might be wary of perks such as these, which could be pointing to such a corporate culture. Perks are only one glimpse inside a company's culture, so be sure to do your research before you jump to any conclusions.

- Fitness-related points programs where employees are rewarded for activities such as participating in running and walking campaigns. Employees then redeem the points for fitness items, such as running shoes, golf clubs, and jogging strollers.

- Paid leave for special traveling or service projects. For example, Patagonia, the outdoor-apparel maker, gives employees two weeks of full-paid leave to work for the green nonprofit of their choice.

- In-house educational programs and other perks are open to relatives of employees.

- Brainstorming allowances, whereby employees are permitted to spend up to 10 percent of their time on research projects of their own devising.

It's important for you to consider which perks would complement your lifestyle and your needs and choose accordingly. If you don't plan on having children for a while, it's not that important whether on-site childcare is offered. Parents, on the other hand, should check to see if the company provides paid time off when a child is sick. If you're not a morning person, ask about flexible hours. If you can't stand wearing a suit, ask about the dress code.

It's important to ask about perks, too, because not all will be offered to all employees, nor will they be mentioned during an interview. The perks that a company offers tells you something about what they value—another insight into the company culture. As you read earlier, it is important to find a company that meshes with your goals, interests, and needs.

SO, HOW MUCH WILL YOU MAKE?

It's tricky to say exactly what you should expect to earn when you first enter the market, because web design salaries vary widely, especially among independent contractors. As you read earlier, your salary will depend greatly on where in the country you work and

Check out the U.S. Bureau of Labor Statistics website for the latest and greatest salary data.

the subsequent cost of living there. It's in your best interest to do your homework and research the cost of living in the area you're considering, and to become familiar with the competitive starting salaries there—all before you're made an offer.

In general, web designers are able to make a decent living. According to salary.com, the median salary for web designer is $62,913. The median wage is the wage at which half the workers in an occupation earned more than that amount and half earned less. Fifty percent of web designers make between $55,377 and $71,903 per year. According to the Bureau of Labor Statistics, the median annual wage for web developers was $62,500 in May 2012 (most recent data available). The lowest 10 percent earned less than $33,550, and the top 10 percent earned more than $105,200. These salaries include beginners and those who are highly experienced, so you're not likely to start there.

As a comparison, the annual AIGA/Aquent Survey of Design Salaries from the Minneapolis School of Advertising, Design & Interactive Studies cites a median total compensation of $38,500 for "junior" web designers in 2012. According to several other sources, the average starting salary for web designers ranges from $24,324 to $43,385. It's a great position to enter at the ground level, salary wise.

To get a more accurate and updated range of starting salaries, search for "junior web designer salary." You'll likely see offerings more in the range of $30,000 to $45,000. Check out the U.S. Bureau of Labor Statistics site as well, which culls governmental data into easy-to-read charts and data points (bls.gov/ooh/computer-and-information-technology/web-developers.htm).

Can you negotiate your salary? If this is truly your first job, the short answer is no. With little experience and being "low on the totem pole," you're not likely to be in the position to negotiate a better salary. If you have some extraordinary experience, or something that is particularly desired by this specific company, you may be the exception. However, most companies, particularly large and mid-sized, have standard packages that they offer to newbies and they don't stray very far from those offerings. If you feel that you have something extraordinary to offer, you may have more luck negotiating better benefits or perks, such as a greater number of vacation days or access to the tuition-reimbursement program much sooner than it's normally offered.

INCREASING YOUR ODDS OF SUCCESS

You should now have a much better idea about what website designers do and how you can become one. If you're still interested in a career in web design, congratulations! To increase your odds of success along the way, keep these points in mind:

- **Start building your portfolio now.** You can start by developing a personal website or blog using free tools on the Internet. Practice and learn as much as you can.

- **Educate yourself.** Whether it's about the market, the technologies, the schools, or the companies, do the research. Be "in the know." You'll make better decisions and give better interviews.

- **Be positive but realistic.** The market for website designers is competitive, and working for others can be

Perhaps the easiest road to success is to discover your passion and do that for a living.

trying at times. If you have a passion for the work, you can and will succeed.

- **Build your interpersonal communication skills.**
  No matter what you end up doing for a living, you'll do it better when you can deal with people calmly and positively.

- **Find a company whose culture matches your interests.** When you believe in what you're doing, it makes everything easier.

Above all else, discover your passion and live it. This is sometimes easier said than done, but if you accomplish it, your work will never seem like drudgery, and you'll be a happier person. Good luck in your career search!

GLOSSARY

Adobe Dreamweaver A design package by Adobe Systems that enables the HTML programmer to build complex interactive websites using HTML, JavaScript, and server-side programming languages.

Adobe Illustrator A design program developed and marketed by Adobe Systems. Website designers use it to create what is typically called outline art, which includes logos, buttons, or custom lettering that they can't create in Photoshop.

Adobe InDesign A desktop publishing software application produced by Adobe Systems. Designers use it to create works such as posters, flyers, brochures, magazines, newspapers, and books.

Adobe Photoshop A graphics-editing program developed and published by Adobe Systems. Website designers use it to create artwork for placement on websites.

blog Personal websites that users create to record and share frequent (often daily) opinions, musings, stories/poems, links, and so on.

CAPTCHA (Completely Automated Public Turing Test to tell Computers and Humans Apart) A program that can generate and grade tests that humans can pass but current computer programs cannot. CAPTCHA uses small graphics that cannot be read by computer-automated spammers and the like. They are used to verify that data entered into a website (such as registration attempts, blog responses, and online poll responses) is coming from an actual human user and not from attack and spam "bots."

content management systems (CMS) Programs, such as WordPress and Joomla!, that website designers and developers use to manage the content of their websites. They enable designers to create and edit websites without needing a webmaster.

Cascading Style Sheets (CSS) A standard style sheet language that designers use to control the look and formatting of documents created in markup languages, such as HTML, to be displayed on the web as websites. Use of CSS separates style from content, which enables designers to provide more flexibility and control over how information is displayed, regardless of the browser used. CSS can even allow the same markup page to be presented in different styles for different rendering methods, such as on mobile devices.

Drupal A free, open source CMS program that can be used by individuals or groups of website designers to create and manage many types of websites. The application includes a content management platform and a development framework. Claims to be easy to use and good for beginners lacking technical skills.

HTML (Hypertext Markup Language) The markup language that uses tags, such as <h1> and <style>, to create web pages.

interface design A type of design that fully encompasses traditional human–computer interaction, and extends it by addressing all aspects of a product or service as perceived by its users.

intranet Local, restricted, web-like sites, usually created and maintained by a company or organization for the purposes of communicating privately with its employees or members.

GLOSSARY

JavaScript An object-oriented, client-side computer programming language used to create interactive effects on websites. JavaScript is most often used to create client-side scripts that interact with users and control the content that's displayed, depending on information coming from the user's browser. Its uses include validating forms, showing/hiding elements dynamically, creating animations, and communicating with the server in the background.

Joomla! A free, open source content management system based on PHP. It's known for its powerful extensions, and for how well it manages different user permissions.

open source program Software that can be freely used, changed, and shared by anyone and has been created under the Open Source License.

PHP A free server-side scripting language designed for web development and released under the PHP License. Although PHP originally stood for Personal Home Page, it now stands for PHP: Hypertext Preprocessor.

responsive design Website design that is created to respond to the user's device type and display a version that's appropriate for that device. The website code recognizes which device the viewer is using to access it (laptop, smartphone, or tablet, for example) and responds by providing the version of the website that's been designed just for that device.

SaaS (Software as a Service) A model of software distribution where users access the software from a "cloud" (a network of remote servers), rather than have a copy of the software on their local devices. Also called cloud computing.

search engine optimization (SEO) Designing a website so that the results positively affect its visibility in a search engine's "natural" or unpaid search results.

typography Describes the style and appearance of printed material, including text and graphics.

user experience design Design that fully encompasses traditional human–computer interaction, and extends it by addressing all aspects of a product or service as perceived by its users. Sometimes also called user-centered design.

web graphic design Design that focuses on the graphical aesthetics of a website, including web page layout.

webmaster A person who creates and manages information on websites, and/or manages the computer server and technical aspects of website programming.

WordPress The most popular blogging system in use on the web, WordPress is a free and open source blogging tool and a content management system based on PHP. It runs on a web hosting service and has a plug-in architecture and a template system.

World Wide Web Consortium (W3C) Led by web inventor Tim Berners-Lee, W3C is an international community that works together with the public to develop standards for the web.

SOURCE NOTES

INTRODUCTION

(1) pg. 7: Cookson, Paul, "Goodreads," www.goodreads.com/ quotes/tag/web-design.

(2) pg. 9: Spool, Jared. *Web Site Usability: A Designer's Guide*. (San Francisco, CA: Morgan Kaufmann Publishers, 1998), p. 62.

CHAPTER 1

(1) pg. 15: "Cisco Global Mobile Data Traffic Forecast, 2013–2018," Cisco.com, www.cisco.com/c/en/us/solutions/collateral/ service-provider/visual-networking-index-vni/VNI-Forecast_ QA.html.

(2) pg. 22: Rowling, J.K. *Harry Potter and the Chamber of Secrets*. (New York, NY: Author A. Levine Books, 1999), p. 333.

(3) pg. 24: "Usage Statistics and Market Share of Content Management Systems for Websites," W3Techs, w3techs.com/ technologies/overview/content_management/all

(4) pg. 24: Coalo, J.J. "With 60 Million Websites, WordPress Rules the Web. So Where's The Money?" *Forbes*, September 5, 2012. p. 3.

(5) pg. 24: "Leadership Highlights," *The Joomla! Community Magazine*, magazine.joomla.org/issues/Issue-Apr-2012/item/736-Leadership-Highlights-from-March-2012.

(6) pg. 25: "Usage Stats for January 2013," The PHP Group, php. net/usage.php.

(7) pg. 25: "The Open Source Definition," The Open Source Initiative, opensource.org/osd.

(8) pg. 26: "Occupational Outlook Handbook: Web Developers," U.S. Bureau of Labor Statistics, 2012 data, bls.gov/ooh/ computer-and-information-technology/web-developers.htm.

CHAPTER 2

(1) pg. 30: "Occupational Outlook Handbook: Web Developers."

(2) pg. 31: Dunn, Sam, "The Role of College for Web Designers," Build Internet by One Mighty Roar, buildinternet. com/2009/12/the-role-of-college-for-web-designers.

(3) pg. 32: "Analysis Finds Wide Wage Disparities Among Virginia College Grads," collegemeasures.org/post/2012/11/Analysis-Finds-Wide-Wage-Disparities-Among-Virginia-College-Grads. aspx.

(4) pg. 34: "Web Designer Training," Computer Training Schools, computertrainingschools.com/career-training/web-designer.

 (5) pg. 34: "Web Authoring Using Dreamweaver," Adobe.com, adobe.com/education/resources/certificate-programs/ dreamweaver-exam-objectives.edu.html?.

(6) pg. 39: "Education/Students," Adobe.com, adobe.com/ education/students.edu.html?showEduReq=no.

SOURCE NOTES

(7) pg. 40: "About Vitaly Friedman," *Smashing Magazine*, smashingmagazine.com/author/vitaly-friedman.

(8) pg. 40: "Cameron Moll," cameronmoll.com.

(9) pg. 41: "Jakob Nielsen," nngroup.com/people/jakob-nielsen.

(10) pg. 41: "Veerle Pieters," veerle.duoh.com.

(11) pg. 41: "Dave Shea," mezzoblue.com/about/dave.

(12) pg. 43: Snell, Steve, "Group Interview: Expert Advice for Students and Young Web Designers," *Smashing Magazine*, smashingmagazine.com/2010/02/17/group-interview-advice-for-students-and-new-designers.

(13) pg. 45: Snell, "Group Interview: Expert Advice for Students and Young Web Designers."

CHAPTER 3

(1) pg. 51: "Career Personality and Aptitude Test," *Psychology Today*, psychologytoday.tests.psychtests.com/take_test.php?idRegTest=3242.

(2) pg. 60: "10 Things You Didn't Know About Working for a Nonprofit," *NY Daily News*, nydailynews.com/jobs/10-didn-working-nonprofit-article-1.348982.

(3) pg. 59: "Occupational Outlook Handbook: Web Developers."

(4) pg. 63: Pieters, Veerle, "Veerle's Blog: Creativity Catalyst and Design Inspiration," veerle.duoh.com/about.

(5) pg. 64: "The Creative Momentum," thecreativemomentum.com.

(6) pg. 64: "Perfect Search Design," perfectsearchdesign.com.

(7) pg. 64: "Blue Fountain Media," bluefountainmedia.com.

(8) pg. 64: "Clikzy Creative," clikzy.com.

(9) pg. 64: "Forix Web Design," forixwebdesign.com.

(10) pg. 65: "Isadora Design," isadoradesign.com.

CHAPTER 4

(1) pg. 70: "Compare Cost of Living," FindTheBest.com, cost-of-living.findthebest.com.

(2) pg. 71: "Vacations, Holidays, and Personal Leave: Access, Quantity, Costs, and Trends," U.S. Bureau of Labor Statistics, www.bls.gov/opub/perspectives/issue2.pdf.

(3) pg. 71: "Vacations, Holidays, and Personal Leave: Access, Quantity, Costs, and Trends."

(4) pg. 73: Chapman, Cameron, "Some Reasons You Might Not Want To Become a Web Designer," Noupe.com, noupe.com/freelance/some-reasons-you-might-not-want-to-become-a-web-designer.html.

(5) pg. 77: "Web Designer Salaries," Salary.com, www1.salary.com/Web-Designer-Salary.html.

(6) pg. 77: "Occupational Outlook Handbook: Web Developers."

SOURCE NOTES

(7) pg. 77: "AIGA/Aquent Survey of Design Salaries 2012," The Minneapolis School of Advertising, Design & Interactive Studies, braincomsa.com/aiga-aquent-survey-of-design-salaries.

(8) pg. 77: "Web Designer Salaries," Salary.com, www1.salary.com/Web-Designer-Salary.html.

(9) pg. 78: "Junior Web Designer Salaries," Simply Hired, simplyhired.com/salaries-k-junior-web-designer-jobs.html.

FURTHER INFORMATION

BOOKS

Boulton, Mark. *A Practical Guide to Designing for the Web.* Penarth, Wales: Mark Boulton Design Ltd., 2009.

Heller, Steven, and Teresa Fernandes. *Becoming a Graphic Designer: A Guide to Careers in Design*, 4th ed. Hoboken, NJ: John Wiley & Sons, 2010.

Lopuck, Lisa. *Web Design for Dummies*, 3rd ed. Hoboken, NY: John Wiley & Sons, 2012.

Robbins, Jennifer Niederst. *Learning Web Design: A Beginner's Guide to HTML, CSS, JavaScript, and Web Graphics*, 4th ed. Sebastopol, CA: O'Reilly Media, 2012.

Teens' Guide to College & Career Planning. Lawrenceville, NJ: Peterson's Publishing, 2011.

WEBSITES

Mapping Your Future
www.mappingyourfuture.org

Discover more about what you want to do and map out a path to reach your career goals. Learn helpful tips on résumé writing, job-hunting, and job interviewing.

FURTHER INFORMATION

Monster

www.monster.com

Perhaps the most well known and certainly one of the largest employment websites in the United States. You can sort by job title as well as by company name, location, salary range, experience range, and much more. The site also includes information about career fairs, advice on résumé writing, interviewing, and more.

Occupational Outlook Handbook

www.bls.gov/oco

Produced by the U.S. Bureau of Labor Statistics, this website offers lots of relevant, updated information about various careers including average salaries, how to work in the industry, the job's outlook in the job market, typical work environments, and what workers do on the job.

Smashing Magazine

www.smashingmagazine.com

This online magazine delivers useful and innovative information to web designers and developers. Their aim is to inform their readers about the latest trends and techniques in web development. A well-respected and extremely popular place to visit, learn from, and bookmark. The site boasts over 130,000 RSS subscribers and is hosted on seven servers.

TUTORIALS AND ONLINE CLASSES

Code Cademy

www.codecademy.com

At Code Cademy (no "A"), you can learn how to code in JavaScript, PHP, HTML/CSS, jQuery, and more, by practicing. You learn by following the tutorial. Upon completion, you have actually created something, such as an animation or a real website. You do have to create an account in order to access the tutorials. This site also has a community aspect. When you join, you can connect with other designers and coders and exchange ideas and ask questions.

w3Schools

www.w3schools.com

Self-named "the world's largest web development site," this website offers free online step-by-step tutorials in HTML, CSS, JavaScript, PHP, and more. Tutorials build on skill and knowledge, and are targeted for beginners all the way to experts. They also have web-building demos where you can learn to create websites on your own computer.

BIBLIOGRAPHY

"10 Things You Didn't Know About Working for a Nonprofit." *NY Daily News*, July 8, 2008. Accessed March 26, 2014. www.nydailynews.com/jobs/10-didn-working-nonprofit-article-1.348982.

"Career Personality and Aptitude Test." *Psychology Today*. Accessed March 26, 2014. psychologytoday.tests.psychtests. com/take_test.php?idRegTest=3242.

Chapman, Cameron. "Some Reasons You Might Not Want To Become a Web Designer." Noupe.com, August 17, 2010. Accessed April 2, 2014. noupe.com/freelance/some-reasons-you-might-not-want-to-become-a-web-designer.html.

Lopuck, Lisa. *Web Design for Dummies*, 3rd ed. Hoboken, NJ: John Wiley & Sons, 2012.

"Occupational Outlook Handbook: Web Developers." U.S. Bureau of Labor Statistics, 2012 data. Accessed March 17, 2014. www.bls.gov/ooh/computer-and-information-technology/web-developers.htm.

Snell, Steve. "Group Interview: Expert Advice for Students and Young Web Designers." *Smashing Magazine*, February 17, 2010. Accessed March 20, 2014. smashingmagazine.com/2010/02/17/group-interview-advice-for-students-and-new-designers.

Spool, Jared. *Web Site Usability: A Designer's Guide*. San Francisco, CA: Morgan Kaufmann Publishers, 1998.

Teens' Guide to College & Career Planning. Lawrenceville, NJ: Peterson's Publishing, 2011.

"Vacations, Holidays, and Personal Leave: Access, Quantity, Costs, and Trends." U.S. Bureau of Labor Statistics. Accessed April 2, 2014. bls.gov/opub/perspectives/issue2.pdf.

INDEX

Page numbers in **boldface** are illustrations.

ABOUT THE AUTHOR

KEZIA ENDSLEY is an editor and author from Indianapolis, Indiana. She has been involved in the technical publishing field since the days of CompuServe, before the "real" Internet took off. She has, over two decades, enjoyed being a part of educating people of all ages about technical subjects. In addition to editing technical publications and writing books for teens, she enjoys running and triathlons, reading, and spending time with her family and her cats.